Original title:
Where the Walls Meet the Sky

Copyright © 2025 Creative Arts Management OÜ
All rights reserved.

Author: Tobias Sterling
ISBN HARDBACK: 978-1-80587-221-4
ISBN PAPERBACK: 978-1-80587-691-5

Unity in Dissonance

In the land of mismatched socks,
We dance on hopes and silly clocks.
The laughter echoes through the halls,
As we trip on fate and tumblefalls.

A cat in a hat claims the throne,
While dogs in shades strut with a moan.
With every quirk that we embrace,
We find sweet joy in our wild grace.

The Language of Elevation

Birds write letters with their beaks,
While squirrels debate the future weeks.
In the chatter of a bustling hive,
We giggle as the bees connive.

The clouds are having a tea party,
Splashing raindrops, oh so hearty.
With each flutter and winged jest,
We taste the air—it's quite the fest!

Convergence of Dreams

A pig in a tutu leads the show,
While cows in sneakers put on a glow.
We gather here, a wacky crew,
Unraveling tales, both old and new.

Dreams collide like bouncing balls,
As whispers float through paper walls.
The moon chuckles, joining the fun,
As we chase shadows, one by one.

A Symphony of Peaks and Valleys

The mountains hum a tuneful tease,
While valleys sway with utmost ease.
Together they create a song,
Of silly moments, right or wrong.

Frogs in top hats sing with glee,
As bees conduct with wild decree.
In this orchestra of height and depth,
We find our rhythm with each misstep.

Wisps of the High Above

Fluffy clouds with silly grins,
Dance around where day begins.
A pigeon dressed in polka dots,
Hangs out near a pot of pots.

The sun plays tag with shadows near,
While squirrels plot a nutty smear.
We giggle at the skies so bright,
As birds do acrobatics in flight.

A Covenant Beyond the Structure

Rooftops chat, a gossip spree,
While antennas say, 'Look at me!'
The moon winks with a crescent cheer,
And chimneys puff out jokes, oh dear!

The wind whirls tales of wayward kites,
As neighbors on their balconies fight.
Fences tremble with laughter's call,
In the union of the tall and small.

The Intersection of Dreams and Reality

At dawn the dreams like bubbles float,
While cats in hats pretend to goat.
A dreamer snoozes in a tree,
While reality plays hide and seek.

Pint-sized creatures plot their flair,
Mice in slippers dance with care.
The sun yawns wide, saying 'Hey,
Let's mix dreams with a splash of play!'

Threads of the Skyline

Kites of laughter fly on high,
While weaves of threads are fruitcake pie.
Kangaroos in coats of blue,
Jump through rainbows just for you.

A giraffe steals a donut swirl,
Balloons float high with giggles, twirl.
The rooftops wear a silly crown,
In a city where the fun's the town.

The Arc of Dreams

In a town where llamas wear hats,
And cats play chess with the bats,
We build our dreams with spaghetti strands,
While juggling marshmallows with our hands.

Above us, clouds do silly tricks,
Like acrobats tossing grinning bricks,
As rainbows slide down the rainbow slide,
We giggle and laugh on this dream ride.

Where Dreams Touch Infinity

A turtle in a bowtie struts,
While squirrels in suits plan their cuts,
We dance on clouds made of cotton candy,
With upbeat tunes from a frog band, dandy!

The stars are winking, playing charades,
While moonbeams shine through lemonade shades,
In this realm of whimsy and cheer,
Every giggle floats, bright and clear.

An Elevation of Thought

We launched our thoughts on paper planes,
They soared like birds with silly gains,
Scribbles flutter through the sunny beams,
Turning into laughter-filled dreams.

As carrots chat with dancing bees,
And zebras play hopscotch with ease,
In the heights where giggles ignite,
Each thought takes off, reaching new height.

Synthesis of the Far and Near

In a land where chairs play charades,
And spoons sit courtside for parades,
We mix and mash the absurd and sweet,
Stirring up smiles, a delightful feat.

The sun wears sunglasses, oh so bright,
While trees groove gently, feeling light,
In this blend of the strange and fun,
Every moment's a laugh, never done.

Tapestry of Earth and Air

Balloons and kites dance in the breeze,
A squirrel on a branch sneezes with ease.
In shoes too big, a child does prance,
While ants are throwing a tiny dance.

Laughter spills over the garden wall,
As goats play tag, heedless of the call.
The sun yawns wide, brushes the trees,
While a cat curiously checks the bees.

The Calm Above the Chaos

A pigeon in a bowtie surveys the scene,
While pigeons gossip of who's benevolent and mean.
A dog walks past, wearing sunglasses low,
Who knew city pets put on such a show?

Meanwhile, the clouds are having a feast,
Dropping rain like confetti from a beast.
Beneath it all, we giggle and sigh,
As umbrellas flip inside out with a cry.

Haze Between Realms

In my backyard, a portal spins and whirls,
Socks and sandals defy gravity's curls.
An alien asked for ketchup on fries,
While I just stared with wide-open eyes.

The garden gnomes have thrown a rave,
With disco balls made from a walnut shell grave.
They beckon me to join in the fun,
But I just grin and call it a pun.

Portal of the Infinite

A toaster pops up with a gleeful ding,
Proclaiming it's time for breakfast to sing.
With waffles floating, they dart to my plate,
As syrup rivers create a sticky fate.

The cat tried to fish in a screen on the wall,
Jumping up high, he took quite a fall.
Pancakes giggled, 'Let's switch it around,'
As I, the chef, danced all over the ground.

Ascent to the Untamed Vault

On my roof, I took a leap,
Into clouds, that fluffy heap.
Tripped on air, did a twirl,
Pretending I could fly and whirl.

Gravity laughed with a snicker,
While I came down—oh, how quicker!
My landing was a sight to see,
A dance of joy—oh, woe is me!

I scolded the sky for being so high,
But it winked back, a cheeky eye.
Next time I'll bring a trampoline,
And bounce until I'm truly seen!

With rooftops round, my kingdom's crown,
I'll host my friends, no skyward frown.
We'll throw confetti, paper, and dreams,
And jump so high, or so it seems.

Fractured Skies and Concrete Heartbeats

In the city, a pigeon did glare,
Why do humans think they can share?
Their lofty dreams and grander plans,
While I just peck at crumbs from cans.

Concrete heartbeats thrum below,
As I dodge a pizza slice in flow.
Look, I can dance, oh what delight,
Just not with a kid who can't take flight!

The clouds chuckle with a knowing sound,
As sporks and forks rain from above ground.
Oh, how I laugh at urban misfit tales,
While sipping my coffee from plastic pails.

Beneath those clouds, my shenanigan spree,
With height and humor, just wait and see.
I'll jiggle and waddle, dance on the line,
And claim this neighborhood as truly mine!

Constellations in Concrete

Under bridges, I seek my fate,
Mapping stars on a rusty crate.
The moon giggles, the sun rolls its eyes,
As I sketch out my cosmic pies.

Cement rivers curl with flair,
Scribbled stars sit with a glare.
I jump to reach a cosmic munch,
But instead, I land in a trashy brunch.

Oh, how the planets dance in glee,
For I'm just a dreamer, wild and free.
With each misstep, I lose my grace,
Spilling my dreams all over the place.

But fears can't stop this cosmic show,
Even if my snacks are never to go.
With laughter and joy, I'll paint the night,
Creating constellations filled with delight!

Skyline Reflections

Mirrored buildings laugh and smile,
Reflecting my antics for a while.
I prance along the glassy lane,
Hoping the wind won't cause a strain.

As the skyline gives a wink or two,
I attempt to buy a coffee brew.
But spilled it all upon my shoe,
Now I'm sticky — what's a soul to do?

The rooftops whisper secrets fine,
Of curious cats and urban wine.
I jive and glide with silly flair,
Turning upstairs into a fair so rare.

So come outside, join my spree,
We'll dance past dusk, just you and me.
With laughter echoing in the city's sigh,
We'll paint the horizon — oh my, oh my!

The Sky's Resilient Border

In a world of flapping banners,
Cats wear capes and dance with glee.
While pigeons plot on garden planters,
The sun shows up for tea at three.

Ladders lean against the clouds,
Painted with the laughter of the breeze.
While squirrels scream their circus vows,
Acrobats swing from leafy trees.

The grass whispers tales of flights,
While flowers joke about their height.
A butterfly in colorful tights
Claims the garden's crown with pride.

Above the rooftops, dreams take wing,
As gnomes debate their favorite chime.
With kettles whistling, clouds do sing,
Our frothy thoughts with giggles rhyme.

Reaching for the Unseen

I stretch my arms to catch a cloud,
And toddlers laugh, they think it's cool.
The adult says, 'don't be too loud',
As if the sky is just a school.

Jumping high, I touch a tree,
But squirrels snicker and tease my shoe.
How can they climb so easily?
I blame their training in the zoo.

Invisible stars play hide and seek,
While owls roll their eyes in the night.
Adventurous dreams, so wild and sleek,
Make every wish a fleeting kite.

With rubber bands and paper planes,
We plot our journey to the moon.
But gravity pulls on silly chains,
And down we fall, quite out of tune.

A Serenade of Heights

Upon the rooftops, pigeons croon,
While chimney pots wear hats so tall.
Birdsong weaves a sweet cartoon,
As winds give whispers to us all.

A cloud drifts by, a fluffy friend,
Who tickles trees with laughter light.
He rolls away, as if to send
A message lost in pure delight.

Raccoons in tuxedos hold a ball,
While moles juggle crumbs from nearby pies.
And in the chaos, a silly thrall
Winks at the sun with tiny sighs.

Bicycles race the breezes bold,
As flowers wear their best attire.
The humor here is pure and gold,
As life and laughter lift us higher.

The Junction of Earth and Ether

At twilight's edge, the world unspools,
With squirrels debating cheese and grapes.
The clouds, they giggle, acting fools,
While moonbeams hide behind their capes.

Grasshoppers dance with feathered flair,
While worms play peek-a-boo with worms.
Kites dip low, with tales to share,
Of balloon rides on the wormy terms.

The clouds conspire with silly faces,
As rainbows jump from one to the next.
Weaving stories of far-off places,
In a language all of them perfected.

And here at dusk, the laughter swells,
Hummingbirds giggle at the sight.
With jests as bright as evening bells,
The earth and ether share their light.

The Tapestry of Heights

In a world where pigeons strut,
Sipping coffee from a nut,
The rooftops laugh, they know the game,
As cats parade without a shame.

Ladders lean into the air,
Boys in capes begin to dare,
To jump from dreams and land in fun,
While neighbors wonder who's undone.

Cranes dance salsa with delight,
Construction workers cheer the height,
They trade their hats, they trade their tunes,
As walls collide with sunny moons.

The sun peeks in, the skies bright blue,
A friendly wave from clouds to you,
And laughter ripples through the tiles,
As gravity forgets its trials.

Silent Conversations with the Wind

The breeze whispers secrets low,
To the rooftops, all aglow,
It tickles trees with playful glee,
And nudges hats from folks like me.

Windows creak with tales to tell,
As squirrels scamper, rings the bell,
They gossip about the birds' flight tricks,
While umbrellas dance in cheeky kicks.

Voices float from streets below,
"Is that a cat or just a show?"
The wind just chuckles, free and clear,
As if it knows what we don't hear.

Pigeons think they run the street,
In feathered suits and fancy feet,
But whispers swirl above their heads,
With laughter hiding in their beds.

Skylines in the Golden Hour

The sun's a jester, bright and bold,
Painting rooftops red and gold,
While shadows stretch in silly poses,
And rooftops wear the day's sweet roses.

Laughter echoes through the air,
As people stop with time to spare,
To watch the day do its last dance,
In fading light, they catch a glance.

Buildings sway like sleepy giants,
With windows glinting, quite defiant,
The traffic lights do waltz around,
While happy kids make joyful sound.

In every corner, tales unfold,
Of hurried feet and stories told,
In the golden hour, joy is high,
As laughter floats up to the sky.

Boundaries Embraced by Time

Time tap-dances on old bricks,
With a grin that plays its tricks,
And walls that blush in evening light,
Join the laughter, take to flight.

Neighbors greet with silly jokes,
As laughter spreads like morning smoke,
A garden wall sings the refrain,
"Fences? No! We're just a chain!"

With every tick, a new surprise,
As squirrels ponder, wise and sly,
They gather acorns, twist and twirl,
While time spins on in joyful whirl.

The horizon giggles, wide and free,
As shadows lengthen, it's plain to see,
Boundaries fade, and laughter stays,
In this quirky dance of days.

Whispering Altitudes

In a land where rooftops chat,
And pigeons wear tiny hats,
The clouds all giggle and play,
As the sun ticks time away.

Ladders stretch to tickle clouds,
While kites debate in swirling crowds,
A breeze tells secrets, oh so sly,
As ladybugs zoom through the sky.

Birds form bands up in the blue,
With instruments made of dew,
The horizon cracks a giggle,
As rainbows dance and wiggle.

At twilight, the stars unite,
Telling jokes to the moonlight,
In this place of dreams and fun,
Where laughter threads between everyone.

The Edge of Eternity

Up above, where dreams take flight,
Time wears socks that don't quite fit right,
A clock hangs upside down in the breeze,
Counting laughs lost among the trees.

When clouds wear tufts like fuzzy wigs,
And silly squirrels dance like jigs,
The sun throws a party up high,
With cake made of clouds, oh me, oh my!

In the realm of infinite cheer,
The crickets chirp tunes we hold dear,
Each star a little joke on repeat,
As we chase after the laughter's beat.

Gravity tries but can't keep up,
As giggles spill from every cup,
On this funny edge, forever gleeful,
Finding joys in the most deceitful.

Convergence of Heights

Atop the hills, the silly goats roam,
Wearing sunglasses, feeling at home,
They host tea parties in the air,
With biscuits that've flown, nowhere to share.

Balancing on a wobbly line,
The tightrope walker sips on wine,
He waves to the clouds, bows to the sun,
His show of antics, oh what fun!

Balloons escape with giggles loud,
Joining a parade of a fluffy cloud,
Each float a wish, quite hard to catch,
With wishes like squirrels that all mismatch.

At sunset, they gather to play,
In the twilight's fruity ballet,
With laughter ringing so divine,
This height dance party, simply sublime.

Shadows Against the Celestial Canvas

In twilight's glow, shadows prance,
Creating shapes in a funny dance,
A teapot here, a kangaroo there,
With a moon that giggles at their flair.

Stars throw a party, they twinkle and tease,
As wisps of vapor float on the breeze,
Each laugh a ripple through the night,
Where starlight shines with sheer delight.

The horizon dons a hat of green,
While shadows play hide and seek unseen,
A comet zooms, with a whoosh and a cheer,
As the galaxies laugh in shimmering gear.

With every wink from the darkened space,
And a flicker of joy lighting up our pace,
The cosmos hums a jolly tune,
Under the watch of a joking moon.

Echoes of the Infinite Blue

Clouds float like pancakes, so fluffy and wide,
While birds make their jokes, you can't help but chide.
The sun wears a hat, oh so silly and bright,
As kites dance in circles, a whimsical flight.

Laughter erupts from the ground all around,
As squirrels plot mischief, their antics abound.
The sky's a big canvas, splashed with delight,
Where giggles escape, and dreams take to flight.

Boundaries of Light and Shadow

The sun pulls a prank, it tickles the trees,
Casting long shadows, as if to say, "Cheese!"
While ants hold a meeting, discussing their snack,
The world's a grand stage, but who's playing whack?

Light bounces around like a kid on a spree,
While shadows are giggling at what they can see.
A squirrel steals acorns, then slips on a leaf,
"Do you think I'm a dancer?" it squeaks, in belief.

Horizons Beyond the Brim

The horizon winks back, a fun little tease,
While clouds clap their hands, swaying in the breeze.
A kite, it goes wobbly, a clown in the air,
Tipping its nose, like it just doesn't care.

The stars play hopscotch over mountains so tall,
While planets tell secrets, ensnared by their thrall.
The horizon's a stage, with stardust in tow,
Where laughter and wishes together can grow.

The Meeting Place Above

Up high, there's a party, where all spirits twist,
The moon drops confetti, who could resist?
Planets dance like children, swirling about,
A cosmic charade, filled with laughter and shout.

Stars share their stories, each giggle a spark,
As comets play tag, leaving trails in the dark.
It's a raucous affair, a scattering show,
At the meeting place above, where wonders can flow.

Sanctuary in the Stratosphere

Up on the roof, a goat's on a spree,
Kicking the clouds, just wild and free.
A picnic of cheese, with crackers and foam,
In this heights' abode, we all call home.

Laughter erupts from a squirrel with flair,
Doing a jig with his fluffy brown hair.
A juice box toast, we sip with delight,
To the gravity's pull that just doesn't bite.

Who needs walls when the sky's our quilt?
With stars for the lamps, and moonbeams built.
Dreams float like bubbles, no need for a door,
In our stratosphere playground, we always want more.

As pigeons debate about their flight paths right,
We swing our legs over, giggling with might.
A slip on the ledge, oh what a sight!
Turn the fall into twirls, what pure delight!

A Glimpse Beyond Structure

In my garden of dreams, flowers wear hats,
Waving at clouds, and dodging the bats.
A turtle on crutches marches with glee,
Chasing the breeze, won't catch him, you'll see!

The fence whispers tales of a redheaded crow,
Who thinks he's a parrot, putting on quite a show.
Swinging on rainbows, twirling with flair,
In this ballet of nonsense, light as the air.

Dream catchers wobble, chasing away fears,
While a frog with a trumpet plays jazzy cheers.
The walls shake with laughter, they giggle and sway,
As we dance on the rooftop, come join the fray!

An owl in a tux, so dapper, so wise,
Serves tea to the fireflies blooming like spies.
In this house of façades, we all feel so spry,
For the sky is our ceiling, and laughter our tie.

The Fusion of Heaven and Earth

A cat in a hammock, just lounging around,
While ants on a mission stomp on the ground.
The sun's plotting mischief, its rays are so tight,
Tickling the rooftops and causing a fright.

Bubbles ascend with each giggling burst,
With dreams in them, oh, who could be cursed?
Pigeons as bouncers, guarding our height,
While clouds offer soft beds for a cozy night.

The fence crackles laughter, it creaks with its song,
As we leap from the patio, our hearts feel so strong.
No ceilings here limit the fun we embrace,
In this wonderland, we've all found our place.

The harmony flows like a river in spring,
Where cats with top hats start to dance and to sing.
Underneath every star lies a story untold,
In our cheerful chaos, the universe unfolds.

Veil of the Celestial

Up above in a goofy dance,
The stars do twirl as if in trance.
They trip on comets, slip on light,
Who knew space could be such a sight?

The moon wears socks, a silly sight,
While planets spin, oh what a fright!
Galaxies giggle, swirling near,
A cosmic show that draws us here.

Saturn's rings are hula hoops,
Jupiter's storms are merry troops.
In this vastness, jokes collide,
As laughter echoes far and wide.

So look up high, don't be shy,
Let whimsy drift into your eye.
The heavens jest, they surely will,
Creating smiles from dawn until.

Where Foundations Touch the Clouds

Beneath the beams, the joists hold tight,
A paradox of sheer delight.
Foundations laugh, as ceilings cheer,
Who knew homes had such a sense of queer?

Plumbing pipes joke and sing along,
In every crevice, there's a song.
The wallpaper's got a thing to say,
Whispering tales of yesterday.

Chairs are dancing, with no concern,
While tables wobble, twist, and churn.
In this house of misfit dreams,
Laughter bubbles, or so it seems.

So let your heart be light and free,
Join this crazy jubilee.
In every nook, a chuckle lies,
Accidental joy fills up the skies.

Mirage of the Boundless

In a desert, where shadows play,
Sand dunes laugh in a silly way.
The sun pretends to be a clown,
As mirages tease with their gown.

Cacti joke as they curtsy low,
While tumbleweeds put on a show.
A breeze whispers puns, soft and spry,
Need water? Just look up and sigh.

But lo, the horizon starts to grin,
A playful trick, a cheeky spin.
In this vastness of heat and fun,
Everyone knows, it's all a pun.

So when you wander, take a peek,
And find a chuckle with each shriek.
For in the desert, we all can see,
Endless joy meets the sandy spree.

Chronicles of Air and Stone

Once there lived a rock so bold,
With tales of air that never grow old.
It claimed the clouds were its best pals,
As they shared giddy, happy howls.

Breezes could not stop their chatter,
While stones would roll and giggle, 'What's the matter?'
Each crack in the ground a punchline bright,
Together they laughed, both day and night.

The mountains stood tall, puffing with pride,
Saying, 'We've nothing to hide!'
For nature's jokes echo up and down,
In every valley and every town.

So join in this verse of earth and air,
A symphony of laughter, beyond compare.
In every breeze, a chuckle flows,
As our world dances, in joy it glows.

Journey Beyond the Frame

In a world of paper planes,
I flew through frames of grass,
Chasing squirrels with googly eyes,
And racing pigeons with sass.

Painted clouds in vibrant hues,
Set my dreams out on display,
But they wobbled off the edge,
And promptly flew the wrong way!

The artists nodded, pens in hand,
They sketched me with a grin,
As I tripped on my own shoelace,
And fell into the bin.

With a laugh, I brushed off crumbs,
And found my way once more,
Through frames of joy and giggles,
In the canvas I explore.

Wings of the Urban Canvas

In the city buzz and whirr,
A bird forgot its lunch,
It swooped down, stole my sandwich,
And gave me quite the punch.

The skyscrapers leaned to see,
As I chased that tricky thief,
Through alleys filled with echoes,
And a pigeon stole my belief!

Art sprouted from every street,
With murals that winked so bright,
But the paint cans were all empty,
And I left with paint on my flight!

Yet laughter turned the corner,
In this lively, honking spree,
For in every stolen lunch,
Lies a sense of glee.

Celestial Echoes above Stone

Underneath the twinkling stars,
A cat chased its own tail,
While the moon giggled above,
In a tuneful, bright trail.

The buildings tapped their toes,
To a rhythm quite absurd,
As comets popped like popcorn,
With the softest little word.

Pigeons puffed in harmony,
As they staged their own ballet,
Dancing on the rooftops,
In a funny, feathered play.

With echoes of the night sky,
We sketched our dreams with flair,
For in laughter's boundless reach,
We learn to float in air.

A Landscape of Possibility

In fields of green and purple pizza,
My bike had wings today,
I cycled through a salad bar,
And wished I could just stay.

The sun turned into jellybeans,
Giggles filled the mellow breeze,
As I danced through donut fields,
And chased the wandering bees.

Clouds were pillows, soft and round,
Ready for a funny nap,
But I bounced instead on marshmallow hills,
And fell into a flap!

In this land of endless fun,
Where laughter knows no bounds,
I discovered in each stumble,
A joy that always surrounds.

The Meeting of Dreams and Reality

In a land where socks dance free,
And the cat plays chess with a bee,
Dreams wear hats; oh what a sight,
Reality giggles, trying to take flight.

Bicycles swim in a rosy pond,
While spoons do the tango, and wands respond,
Every elephant wears a bright bow tie,
As we ask, 'Is this truth, or just a pie?'

Waffles sing hymns to the breakfast moon,
While toast debates with a sleepy raccoon,
Cactus plants wear shoes and laugh with glee,
In this crazy realm, let's just let it be.

So bring your thoughts, let's play a game,
In this wacky space, nothing's the same,
As upside down smiles parade in the light,
Come join the riddle, it's pure delight!

Where Nature Kisses the Build

The trees wear hats of urban gray,
While squirrels discuss their plans each day,
Grapevines tango on street lamp poles,
As pigeons gossip about cheeky shoals.

A flower sneezed, oh what a scene,
It showered petals on a metal machine,
Brick walls waltz with ivy's embrace,
In this silly dance, nature finds space.

Loud frogs croak to the traffic tunes,
As sunsets paint the sky with maroon spoons,
Grass giggles as it tickles our toes,
While buildings dream of gardens that grows.

So let's join in this chaotic spree,
Where nature and structure, wild and free,
Create a symphony, hilarious and bright,
In the spot where the green meets the light.

Fragments of the Distant Blue

Up high, balloons argue with birds,
While clouds tell stories, in fluffy words,
The sun wears shades, looks down with pride,
As stars dance around, oh what a ride!

A fish jokes with the moonlight's gleam,
While wandering daisies plot and scheme,
The hills whisper secrets to the breeze,
What a riddle, such a puzzle, oh please!

Laughing shadows skip on the ground,
In the distant blue, joy can be found,
A painted sky drips colors galore,
As painted rocks dream of peace, and more.

So come float with us in this brilliant hue,
Where laughter lights paths, and skies feel new,
In a world that spins in a comical way,
Let's unravel the charm, come out and play!

Twilight's Hand on the Ruins

In ruins where laughter used to dance,
The crumbling walls now plot their romance,
Cacti wear wigs and chase after flies,
While shadows attempt to tell silly lies.

A goblet of dreams, cracked but bright,
Reflects the moon in a candle's light,
Mice play cards with a fortune teller,
As the wind hums tunes, a greatest seller.

Ghostly whispers share jokes of the past,
While owls hold parties, shadows cast,
Every fallen stone has something to say,
In twilight's arms, we dream and play.

So let the night giggle in delight,
As we raise our glasses to the fading light,
In ruins reborn, let's dance with mirth,
For even the old finds joy on this earth!

Celestial Visions

In the clouds a cat does prance,
Wearing boots, it leads a dance.
A cosmic mouse squeaks and darts,
While shooting stars play their parts.

Jupiter's got a noodle stand,
Serving pasta with a grand.
Saturn flips pancakes round and round,
In this space, fun knows no bound.

The moon's a disco ball that twirls,
As comet tails unleash their swirls.
All the planets come to play,
In this wacky Milky Way.

With aliens jiving in bright hues,
The universe is full of news.
They giggle, snicker, laugh aloud,
In the skies, we're all so proud.

Shadows in the Heightened Realm

In a realm where shadows creep,
Silly specters love to leap.
They tickle ghosts that float on by,
While bats perform a theater high.

Spectral jokes echo through the night,
"Boo!" they laugh with all their might.
A haunted house spins in delight,
As phantoms tango, what a sight!

On the rooftops owls hold court,
With their spectacles, they report.
"Who's that knocking on the door?"
"It's just the wind, let's dance some more!"

In the dark, their laughter plants,
Funny pranks of hallowed chants.
They giggle, snort, and then take flight,
In shadows grand, they own the night.

Lament of the Ascended

Up above, the angels sigh,
Playing poker in the sky.
With golden wings, they face their fate,
As they hilariously debate.

"Did you see that cloud pass by?"
One angel quips, "Oh my, oh my!"
Another shakes their head with glee,
"Leave it be, that's just the tea!"

Heaven's choir bursts into song,
With off-key notes they belt along.
"Can you believe we're up this high?
Let's have more donuts, oh my my!"

Their laughter echoes near and far,
Heaven's antics, like shooting stars.
In the clouds, they roam and jest,
In their paradise, they're truly blessed.

Stories Written in Space

Once upon a time in space,
A giraffe wore a goofy face.
With rocket boots, it zoomed around,
In search of silly tales profound.

A bubblegum moon began to pop,
While comets called, "No, don't you drop!"
Monkeys on Mars wrote silly scripts,
About yogurt on cosmic trips.

Stars play charades with flair and wit,
While cosmic bears make laughter fit.
"Tell me more!" a starling cries,
As words like candy fill the skies.

These stories drift from star to star,
In every pocket, near and far.
In the cosmos, fun takes flight,
Telling tales through day and night.

The Dance of Foundation and Flight

The bricks below just waved goodbye,
As clouds above began to sigh.
A dance ensued, both firm and fleeting,
In a jig of joy, the ceiling's greeting.

The beams were bopping, full of cheer,
While rafters laughed, "We have no fear!"
The ground was solid, yet so absurd,
As laughter soared, they twisted and whirled.

The windows winked, with glimmers bright,
As shadows joined the evening light.
From sill to sill, a merry tune,
In the style of a sunbeam's swoon.

The roof might trip on a starlit beam,
A hilarious tumble, how they gleam!
Gravity giggled, too close to the edge,
While gutters grinned, forming a hedge.

In the Presence of the Vast

Oh vast expanse, you stretch and yawn,
A canvas wide at the crack of dawn.
The horizon chuckled, took a glance,
"Why don't you join in for a dance?"

The sky wore stripes of orange and blue,
While clouds played tag, enjoying their view.
The sun stretched wide, a bright-faced clown,
Tickling the edges of the town.

Breezes pranced, with a fluttering flair,
Tickling the branches, without a care.
The mountains giggled, "What a fine show!"
As the valleys chimed in, "Don't be slow!"

From peak to peak, the laughter spread,
Echoing softly where spirits tread.
The sky winked back; no sense of pride,
In the vastness, we share the ride.

The Canvas of the Elevated

In colors bright, let imaginations soar,
As roofs and peaks invite us to explore.
A painter's muse, the heights call true,
With laughter dripping in every hue.

Each brush stroke whispers a friendly jest,
As the breeze joins in like a playful guest.
Windows frame the jokes, a spectacle,
With sill-tales shared, quite fantastical.

The ladder leans out, a balancing act,
While the beams below tease, "What's the pact?"
Oh, to be higher, where the fun does brew,
In antics grand, beneath skies so blue.

A rooftop party, all invitees in,
With shingles cheering, we let the night begin.
Above the chaos, joy rides the crest,
In a canvas of laughter, we are truly blessed.

Secrets of the Elevated Edge

On the ledge, where murmurs reside,
Secrets flutter, they cannot hide.
The wind whispers tales of heights so grand,
Of mischief planned by a daring hand.

A bird perched near, with a wink and a smile,
Shared its wisdom, "Let's stay awhile!"
Feathers and shingles, a quirky team,
As they plotted fun, wrapped in a dream.

The eaves dropped low, with a knowing nod,
Jokes and jests from the radiant pod.
The rooftops giggled, a lively throng,
Woven together, where they belong.

Secrets unfurl in the twilight's embrace,
As the stars appear, joining the race.
On the edge of laughter, where friendship blends,
Life's comedy plays, with no need for amends.

The Meeting of Textures and Tiers

In a house with a funny door,
The ceiling laughed, 'I need more!'
The floor said, 'I hold up a load,'
While the wall just grinned; it's quite the road.

A rug squeaked when folks walked by,
'Don't trip!' it yelled, 'Just aim for the sky!'
The curtains waved like they had a dance,
While the clock went 'tick' with a silly prance.

The table wobbled, very unsure,
'Help me out! I can't take this tour!'
The chair sighed deeply, 'Life's such a jest,'
All while the fridge took a well-deserved rest.

So here they gather, a quirky crew,
Mixing textures, layers, in a hullabaloo!
With laughs echoing through each little space,
Life's a funny romp in this merry place.

Embracing the Infinite

Up on a rooftop, a cat ran wild,
Chasing dreams with the grace of a child.
The chimney chimed, 'Let's have some fun!'
While birds passed overhead, soaring one by one.

A cloud drifted by with a tuft so round,
It giggled softly, 'I'm where joy is found!'
The sun blinked brightly, 'Guess who's in charge?'
Casting shadows so long, they looked quite large.

The dog barked loudly, trying to sing,
Though his pitch was more "oomph" than anything.
A breeze tossed its hair, laughing at this,
While the world spun around in a whimsical bliss.

So here they lie, in a comedy show,
In a space so vast, where wonders flow!
Amongst the giggles, we find our delight,
In this funny realm, all feels just right.

Fragments of Infinite Blue

In a splash of color, the skies went mad,
Puddle reflections made everyone glad.
A paintbrush danced, 'Let's color the day!'
While the clouds threw jokes in a light-hearted fray.

The sun wore shades, looking all cool,
While the moon planned parties, a silvered jewel.
Stars jumped in laughter, twinkling bright,
Saying, 'Join us now, it's a starry night!'

The ocean responded with a giggly wave,
As the shoreline danced, oh how it misbehaved!
The beach ball too, bounced here and there,
Saying, 'Come play, if you dare!'

In this vast expanse, all silliness breeds,
Fragmenting the blues, planting funny seeds.
Where laughter rings out, echoing true,
In the fragments of cobalt, where joy springs anew.

A Realm Above the Edifice

Up high in the tower, a jester took flight,
Making faces with the clouds day and night.
The bricks chuckled softly under the strain,
'We hold it all up, isn't that plain?'

A squirrel in a tie tried to look so grand,
While peering down at the people on land.
He winked from his perch, 'You'll all understand!'
As the wind carried whispers of a joke so bland.

The windows threw shade, playing a trick,
Saying, 'Look, a bird, oh wait, that's a stick!'
While the door, once stoic, broke out in a dance,
Every knock on its frame igniting a chance.

In this realm so lofty, humor runs free,
Layers above layers, a wild jubilee!
Where silliness resonates, echoes and grows,
In this whimsical haven, anything goes!

Beneath the Arching Horizon

Clouds gather round like gossiping friends,
They tickle the sun, leaving shadows in bends.
The ground laughs softly, a tickle to toes,
While kites tell their stories with flamboyant shows.

A dog steals my sandwich, a thief in the park,
With crumbs as the evidence, he leaves quite a mark.
Squirrels throw parties in trees overhead,
While I sit and ponder—I might need some bread.

Birds chirp like comedians under the blue,
They squawk jokes to the clouds, just to break through.
A sunbeam takes a bow, then slips on a shoe,
In this playful world, there's always a new view.

The horizon giggles, it stretches and sways,
As laughter compounds on these whimsical days.
So let's dance with the shadows and sing with the light,
In this silly realm where everything's bright!

Whispering Stones at Dusk

Pebbles tell tales in the twilight's embrace,
They chuckle and chatter, each finds its own pace.
A cat struts on by, wearing wisdom like hats,
While shadows gather for their evening spats.

Moss joins the fun, in its velvety cloak,
It wiggles and giggles, it's quite the old joke.
Stones play charades, with their silence so loud,
As echoes of laughter drift up through the crowd.

Bugs wear tiny glasses to read all the signs,
While crickets tap rhythms that nobody minds.
Even the stars, when they peek through the night,
Can't help but chuckle at this whimsical sight.

So come share a moment, beneath starlit skies,
With stones as our friends, and laughter that flies.
The dusk wraps us gently, in warmth and in cheer,
In this silly, sweet world, it's good to be here!

The Summit of Dreams

Up high on the hill, where the air starts to dance,
The clouds wear their best, in a fanciful trance.
A goat with a crown claims the landscape his own,
As laughter erupts, turning grumbles to groans.

The view brings a tear—of joy, not despair,
As butterflies twirl in the thin mountain air.
A squirrel offers snacks, a feast fit for kings,
While I strike a pose, pretending I have wings.

The rocks form a circle to gossip and cheer,
As mountains give way to the echoes we hear.
"Climb higher!" they say, "There's fun yet to find,
With scenery wild and laughter unkind!"

So here on the peak, in the breeze and the glee,
We weigh our own dreams on a scale made of three.
With every new chuckle, we take one more leap,
In this lofty adventure, where joy runs so deep.

Embrace of Earth and Ether

Grass tickles my feet, while daisies debate,
They argue in whispers, but never too late.
A worm in a tie gives a speech like a pro,
While ants march in line, putting on quite the show.

The breeze tells a joke, it swirls round my head,
As butterflies flutter, in colors widespread.
A flower jokes back, with a wink and a sway,
It's a riot down here, at the end of the day.

Mountains chuckle softly, with crags full of glee,
As clouds pass overhead, all fluffy and free.
Nature's hilarity bursts through every seam,
In this playful embrace, it's a chuckler's dream.

So laugh with the earth, let your worries all fly,
While ether wraps round you, like a joyful sigh.
In the warmth of this moment, explore with delight,
Where the charms of the world keep the spirit so bright!

The Union of Elements

In a place where clouds can trip,
The sun slips on a banana peel.
The earth chuckles, while winds do flip,
Water waves say, "That's the deal!"

Fire giggles, melting the ice,
It dances quick, oh what a sight!
While thunder rumbles, not so nice,
Lightning snorts, it's quite the fright!

Air whispers secrets, oh so sly,
As raindrops fall, they start to sing.
A leaf floats by with a wink in its eye,
Nature's circus enjoys the spring.

And when the colors start to play,
Painted skies to seal this show,
The world erupts, let's shout hooray!
For this union, let's go with the flow!

Threshold of Day and Night

When morning stretches, yawns so wide,
The night slips by like a sly cat.
The sun dons shades, with lots of pride,
While moon just grins, 'Hey, how 'bout that?'

Stars dawdle, saying, "Not quite yet!"
While roosters crow, they sound a joke.
The twilight laughs, it's hard to bet,
'Night's got jokes, and day's a bloke.'

Dusk plays tricks, with shadows nice,
Day trips over its own two feet.
Chasing the sun? It's all a dice!
As laughter rings, from dusk to heat.

And when they clash, it sparks a scene,
A comedy on a cosmic throne.
The universe beams in colors keen,
For both of them, it's a merry tone!

The Portrait of Ambition

An artist dreams of skies to climb,
With brushes dipped in rainbow schemes.
But canvases nag him all the time,
"Less coffee, more of those wild dreams!"

He stretches wide, with hues so bright,
Painting success in vibrant drawers.
Yet every stroke just feels too tight,
As ladders reach but still find flaws.

The muse teases with a daring twist,
With failure's grin, they make a pair.
"Eureka!" he shouts, in an artist's mist,
While easels laugh; it's quite a flair!

So he splashes paint, through night and day,
Every canvas tells a silly tale.
In ambition's portrait, fun's at play,
For life's a joke, and dreams won't fail!

Canvassed by the Cosmos

Stars gather round for a cosmic feast,
With planets dancing, what a spree!
They laugh and twirl, not one a beast,
While comets race for all to see.

A black hole grins, with secrets deep,
As stardust sprinkles, soft and light.
Yet somehow, they can't help but leap,
Space-time giggles, what a delight!

Nebulas squabble over colors bold,
While swirling galaxies form a line.
"Hey look!" they shout, "We're hard to hold!
In this art show, we all intertwine!"

And when the universe takes a bow,
Asteroids chuckle, a playful play.
For in this art, we know just how,
The cosmos makes our night less gray!

The Space Between Limits.

In a land where the rooftops bow,
A cat made a throne of an old plow.
With kings made of cardboard and peas,
They argue with squirrels on the breeze.

The moon seemed to wink and laugh,
As bunnies drew maps of the calf.
Their tails wagged with stories untold,
In a world where the funny unfolds.

Old clocks ticked on with a sigh,
As lizards danced under the pie.
With socks made of watermelon zest,
They tried to out-joke the silly quest.

So here in this space, come abide,
With giggles and hiccups as our guide.
For laughter is found in each crack,
In the space where we never turn back.

Beneath the Lattice of Dreams

Underneath the dreamy beams,
We ride on the backs of our dreams.
A snail in a bowler hat stares,
While dancing on stilts with wild hairs.

Jellybeans drip from the trees,
We dip our toes in the sweet breeze.
With a banjo that strums all the tunes,
We tickle the stars with the moons.

The pumpkins start plotting a game,
As ghosts play charades, quite the fame.
A sheep in pajamas whispers 'Baa!',
Chasing his dreams, galloping far.

So beneath this crooked lattice,
Jokes bounce like a springy practice.
With laughter that fills up the air,
Dreamers united, beyond compare.

A Horizon's Embrace

In a vastness where giggles roam,
The horizon waves, calling us home.
With sandwiches flying through the air,
And clouds turn to popcorn, beware!

Seagulls in sunglasses take flight,
While jellyfish dance in delight.
A bicycle made from cheese and jam,
Cycle through a night with a clam.

As the sun spills lemonade gold,
We squeal at the stories retold.
With laughter so loud it rings true,
Each corner addled with something new.

So glide to the edge, take a peek,
Where horizons embrace, mild and meek.
In a place where whimsy aligns,
And the silly is shaped by the signs.

Echoes of the Infinite

In echoes that bounce off the walls,
We hear laughter when the spaceship calls.
Pigs in bowties are sipping their tea,
And ants form a band, wild and free.

The kittens play tag with chalk drawn lines,
While dandelions dance through the vines.
Each echo carries a riddle so bright,
As mushrooms groove under the moonlight.

A raccoon with dreams of a hat,
Tries to sing with the old alley cat.
With hiccups and giggles tucked tight,
They pulse to the rhythm of stars in flight.

So listen close, hear the cheer,
In echoes of joy that draw near.
For in the laughter we find our way,
To a silly tomorrow where we play.

Embracing the Overhang

Beneath the eaves, I often stand,
With pigeons plotting in their band.
They mock my umbrella, its shape a mess,
As raindrops dance, I can only guess.

My hat becomes a tiny sail,
While squirrels plot their next grand tale.
Each drip, a drip—off noses wide,
I stand here soaked, where I abide.

A cat looks down, without a care,
As I try to dodge a falling hair.
The world above, so filled with glee,
Just not so much, it seems, for me.

Yet laughter swells beneath the grey,
As puddles form a mirror play.
My clumsy dance, a silly sight,
Beneath the overhang, quite alright.

Montage of the Outstretched

Arms wide open, clouds I greet,
Still stuck in these two left feet.
Birds fly by, they laugh, they swoop,
While I'm confused, caught in a loop.

Kites above get tangled tight,
While ice cream drips—oh, what a sight!
I reach for dreams that fly away,
My feet still grounded—who can say?

If I could jump, I surely would,
But gravity says 'hey, not good!'
So here I wave at passing stars,
While catching raindrops in my jars.

The joy of heights, my mind's portrayal,
While squirrels plan their next derail.
Each bobbing head, a cloud parade,
In this montage, I've mislaid.

The Roof between Worlds

In a universe atop a shingle,
My thoughts, like cats, begin to mingle.
A trampoline of dreams to bounce,
While I descend, just a tiny ounce.

A ladder leads to nowhere fast,
With socks that slide and slips amassed.
I wave at neighbors—are they real?
Or figments, dancing in a wheel?

Above me, whispers of the breeze,
Remind me not to act with ease.
I balance up, then tumble down,
And all the stars just burst and frown.

In roofs of chatter, worlds collide,
My heart takes off, it cannot hide.
So I'll embrace this playful tide,
Where silly thoughts and dreams abide.

Surreal Heights of Imagination

With penguins flying from the ridge,
I chase my dreams—oh, what a pledge!
I leap from clouds, I haunt the haze,
In this realm, I'm stuck in a daze.

The moon's a trampoline, I bounce,
While lilies giggle, they pronounce:
'Jump higher still, don't look below!'
While I just laugh and steal the show.

Voices echo from the stars,
As giant marshmallows turn to cars.
I drive around in candy rain,
While jellied rivers tease the sane.

In heights so weird, I tap my shoe,
With thoughts surreal that twist and skew.
In imagination's vast, wild play,
I'll dance with joy 'til break of day.

The Edge of Wonder

I looked up high, quite a surprise,
To find a cloud wearing big pink skies.
It winked at me, said, "What a thrill!"
I thought, "Do I need to pay that bill?"

The birds were laughing, doing their dance,
Said, "Join us now, take a funny chance!"
They tossed me crumbs, I tossed them bread,
A feast of giggles, enough to be fed.

The sun peeked down from its lofty seat,
Said, "Well, isn't this a silly treat?"
With every ray, it tickled my face,
I bounced like a ball, a joyful chase!

So when you look where the tall things stand,
Just know there's humor, a funny band.
In the meetings of bright and blue,
Laughter's the ceiling, oh yes, it's true!

Serene Convergence of Heights

Under laughter-shaped trees, I found a cat,
Wearing a hat, quite round and fat.
He looked at me with a wink and grin,
Said, "Climb up high, let the fun begin!"

The squirrels were plotting a funky dance,
They scurried and twirled, not leaving a chance.
I joined their crew, a misfit parade,
In the grand ballet of the forest glade.

The clouds burst out with a goofy cheer,
"Come dance with us, don't you fear!"
So I leapt from branch to branch with glee,
Who knew the treetops could be so free?

So if you find skies quite beyond your sight,
Just remember the laughter, the feline delight.
In a world where heights seem to play,
There's always a joke waiting to make your day!

Dreaming Beyond the Concrete

In a world of stones, I looked up high,
At pigeons discussing, "Should we fly?"
They fluffed their feathers, and surely debated,
A humorous meeting, so underrated!

The rooftops whispered their old, wise jokes,
While chimneys chimed in with puffs of smokes.
A dance of the city, a whimsical spree,
Who knew concrete felt so free?

The stars came out, wearing shades of light,
"Join our party, it's such a delight!"
With every twinkle and every glow,
They laughed at the streets bustling below.

So when you dream of what's up above,
Remember the giggles of concrete love.
For in the noise, there's humor so sly,
Just take a peek, catch a wink from the sky!

Love Letters to the Air

I wrote a note to the breeze so fine,
"Dear Wind, please stop — your dance is divine!"
It laughed and replied with a zesty swirl,
"Bouncing is fun, let's give it a whirl!"

The butterflies joined in the grand farewell,
Writing sweet letters in whirlwinds they'd dwell.
"Dear clouds, we adore your whimsical seams,
Can you send down a sprinkle of dreams?"

The sun chimed in, with a wink and a nod,
"Send hugs to the flowers, that golden façade!"
While trees stood still, trying hard not to sway,
As they caught all the giggles of the day.

So if you find yourself needing a lift,
Just send a love letter, a gleeful gift.
The air is alive with humor and cheer,
A world where laughter is always near!

www.ingramcontent.com/pod-product-compliance
Lightning Source LLC
Chambersburg PA
CBHW060143230426
43661CB00003B/542